IS PEACE POSSIBLE?

A Historical and Biblical Understanding of Current Events in the Middle East

JONATHAN BERNIS

IS PEACE POSSIBLE?

Is Peace Possible?
A Historical and Biblical Understanding of Current Events in the Middle East

Scriptures identified KJV are taken from the King James Version of the Bible.

Published by Jewish Voice Ministries International
PO Box 31998
Phoenix, AZ 85046-1998

Printed in the United States of America

ISBN 978-0-9821117-3-4

A WANDERING NATION

Since the day God called Abram to leave his father's household and go to a land He would show him, promising this land to him and his descendants as an everlasting possession, the Children of Israel have been a Chosen People inseparably tied to a Chosen Land. Sadly however, for most of their history, the Chosen People have been forced to live outside this land.

During the time of Joseph, Jacob and all his family were driven from the land by a great famine and they settled in Egypt. At first they prospered, but as generations passed they came to be viewed as a threat and were enslaved. After being delivered from bondage and the Exodus, they wandered in the desert for 40 years. Eventually Joshua led them across the Jordan River into the Promised Land. This was about 1400 B.C.

After conquering the land of Canaan, the Israelites lived under the rule of various judges until in the days of Samuel they asked for a king to rule over them. Following the reign of Saul, David and Solomon ushered in a golden age for Israel. It was a time of great prosperity and expansion for the nation. But after the death of Solomon, the kingdom was divided. The Northern Kingdom—made up of 10 of the Tribes became known as the Kingdom of Israel, and the Southern Kingdom (which included Jerusalem)—made up of the Tribes of Judah and Benjamin, (and some from Levi...ordained as the priestly Tribe, the Levites) became known as the Kingdom of Judah.

The northern nation of Israel was conquered by the Assyrians in 722 B.C. and the population was dispersed through the empire. There is no record of them ever returning. This is the origin of the great mystery of the "lost tribes of Israel." In 586 B.C. Nebuchadnezzar and the Babylonians defeated the southern kingdom of Judah and took most of the population to Babylon. The people remained there until seventy years passed, then in 516 B.C. they returned to Jerusalem. Solomon's Temple had been destroyed when the Holy City was captured, and those who returned built a new temple, known as the Second Temple.

The Jewish People lived in the land but under the control of other nations for most of the remaining years before the birth of the Messiah. After Alexander the Great defeated Persia, control of Israel passed to the Greeks. After Alexander's death, the empire was then divided to the Seleucids in Syria. The Maccabean revolt briefly gave Israel self-determination again, but soon the Romans conquered the land as part of the expansion of their empire.

The period of Roman rule was marked by a series of increasingly violent revolts and uprisings. The Jewish People particularly despised having their religion controlled by the Romans, who selected rotating high priests in defiance of the Law given by Moses. Roman legions under Titus destroyed the city of Jerusalem and the Temple in 70 A.D., a direct fulfillment of Jesus' prophecy that *"no stone would be left unturned"* (see Mathew 24:2). The final uprising was the Bar Kochba Revolt in 132-136 A.D., after which six Roman legions crushed the rebellion, and the Jews were dispersed throughout the empire. They were forbidden from entering Jerusalem and for the next nearly 1,900 years, the Jewish People became a wandering nation, separated from their homeland.

During the centuries that followed, grave persecutions followed the Jews wherever they went. They were blamed for causing plagues, falsely accused of using the blood of Christian babies to celebrate Passover, and often referred to as "Christ-killers." Waves of persecution during the Crusades, the Inquisition, and the pogroms killed untold thousands. Yet throughout that time, the Jewish People never lost hope that one day they would return.

"Next year in Jerusalem," was their heart's cry through the centuries.

The dream of returning to their homeland and rebuild it again one day remained, and in the late 1800s thousands of Jewish People began immigrating to Israel, then under control of the Ottoman Turkish empire. They primarily came from Eastern Europe and settled in the land as farmers. Known as the First Aliyah, these early settlers struggled for survival in a hostile environment. Early leaders such as Eliezer Ben Yehuda, who revived the use of Hebrew as a language, helped prepare the way for the Jews to return. Ben Yehuda created a Hebrew dictionary to give Jews from all over the world who came to Israel a common language.

Much of the major funding for Jews to return to Israel and purchase land came from the wealthy Rothschild banking family, particularly Walter Rothschild of England. The family gave millions of dollars by today's standards to provide the means necessary to establish the beginnings of the modern nation of Israel. Without this funding it would not have been possible for the early settlers to survive.

THE BIRTH OF ZIONISM

It wasn't until Theodor Herzl wrote a book called "the Jewish State" in 1896 that the modern movement known as Zionism was born. Herzl was a journalist who covered a famous trial that came to be known as the Dreyfus Affair. A French Jewish army officer named Alfred Dreyfus was falsely accused of selling military secrets to Germany. Evidence implicating the real culprit was suppressed, and false evidence manufactured to ensure his conviction. Herzl was so troubled by the implications to all Jews he ultimately devoted his life to the creation of a Jewish homeland, becoming known as the "visionary of Zionism."

In 1897, Herzl organized the World Zionist Organization, which held its first international conference in Switzerland. He stated after the conference: "At Basel I founded the Jewish state. If I were to say this today, I would be greeted by universal laughter. In five years, perhaps, and certainly in 50, everyone will see it." Herzl, whose words came to pass almost 50 years to the day later, died at age 44 and was buried in Vienna. In 1949 after the establishment of Israel, his remains were moved from Vienna to Mount Herzl in Jerusalem.

One of the biggest milestones leading to the formation of the modern State of Israel is the famous Balfour Declaration of 1917. In a letter written by British Foreign Secretary Arthur Balfour to Baron Walter Rothschild, intended to be transmitted to the Zionist Federation of Great Britain and Ireland, the letter formalized the commitment of the British Cabinet reached on October 31, 1917, to support the creation of a nation of Israel. The letter read in part:

"His Majesty's government view with favour the establishment in Palestine of a national home for the Jewish people, and will use their best endeavours to facilitate the achievement of this object, it being clearly understood that nothing shall be done which may prejudice the civil and religious rights of existing non-Jewish communities in Palestine, or the rights and political status enjoyed by Jews in any other country."

The letter further stated that the declaration is a sign of *"sympathy with Jewish Zionist aspirations."*

Although this important document committed the British government to use its best efforts to bring about the establishment of a Jewish homeland, other events took precedence. The First World War was raging, and their main focus was winning the war in Europe. The situation in the Middle East was a minor concern. However, it was just one month after the Balfour Declaration was issued that British forces under General Edmund Allenby captured Jerusalem from the Turks.

Anticipating the downfall of the Ottoman Empire at the conclusion of the First World War the British and French agreed between themselves on a plan to divide the Middle East after the war. The Sykes-Picot Agreement split up the former lands of the Ottoman Turkish Empire into different zones of control and zones of influence for England and France. As part of that agreement, the Holy Land was to be placed under British control.

The revelation of the secret treaty sparked a firestorm of protest in the Middle East. European diplomats and military officials had been making conflicting and contradictory promises to both Arabs and Jews. When the treaty was published, it unmasked the plans of the European powers to maintain control over the region rather than granting freedom to those peoples, which were being liberated from Turkish control. The British did take control of the Holy Land ruling it as a Mandate, but their commitment to create a Jewish homeland was not well received by the Arabs of the region.

In an attempt to clarify their policy and move forward, the British government issued a series of White Papers, interpreting the Balfour Declaration and laying out plans to implement it. The 1922 White Paper set a quota for Jewish immigration and reduced the area of the Mandate by returning a large portion of it to Arab control. The 1930 White Paper went even further in restricting the number of Jews that would be allowed to return. It contained a threat to terminate immigration entirely if the economic consequences of the influx of Jews could not be limited. The final major White Paper, issued in 1939, rejected the idea of Palestine as either a Jewish or Arab state and called for an independent state instead. It also imposed serious restrictions on land acquisition by Jews. The dream of a homeland was still alive, but it seemed no closer to becoming reality. In the 4,000 years since God promised the land to Abraham and his descendants, they had only occupied the land for approximately 1,400 years. For the other 2,600 they wandered the earth as outcasts and sojourners, without a land to call their own. It appeared that would continue, but major events were about to change everything.

THE HOLOCAUST AND THE REBIRTH OF ISRAEL

Even as England struggled with balancing the conflicting promises they had made to Jews and Arabs regarding the Holy Land, a new threat began looming across Europe. The anti-Semitism that had retreated to the shadows following the Dreyfus Affair returned with a vengeance during the Great Depression. The governments of Europe tottered from the financial strain, and in 1933 a charismatic leader named Adolf Hitler took power in Germany.

Hitler's National Socialist German Workers Party, the Nazis, had attempted to overthrow the German government in the 1920s. While Hitler was serving a jail sentence for his part in the failed coup attempt, he wrote *Mein Kampf* (My Struggle) which laid out his plan to free Germany from "the Jewish peril." Hitler was known to be a strong believer in the fraudulent Protocols of the Elders of Zion. That book, published in Russia in 1903, claimed to be the minutes of secret meetings of Jewish men plotting to take over the world. Though quickly revealed as a thinly disguised forgery, the book was widely accepted by those who hated the Jews and spread quickly in a climate of growing anti-Semitism throughout Europe.

While Hitler worked to rebuild Germany's tattered economy, he also instituted a systematic program of discrimination and isolation against the

Jews. Laws were passed restricting the rights of Jews to work and own property. In 1935 the Nuremberg Laws stripped Jews of their citizenship. Kristallnacht—the night of broken glass—in 1938, unleashed unbridled nationwide violence and terror against the Jews, and is considered the beginning of the Holocaust.

Squads of stormtroopers roamed the streets, looting and destroying thousands of Jewish-owned shops, homes, and synagogues. Dozens of Jews were killed, and thousands more rounded up and placed in concentration camps. It was a chilling preview of what was to come. After World War II started and the Nazis spread their control across Europe, Hitler's attention turned to a "Final Solution" for the "Jewish problem"—the term Hitler used to describe his attitude toward the Jews. Mass extermination camps were set up at places like Auschwitz. Jews were shot, beaten to death and gassed by the thousands. By the time the Allied Forces liberated the death camps in 1945, some six million Jews had been murdered.

Following the war, Europe lay in ruins. Even the victorious nations like England and France had suffered enormous financial, structural, and military losses. None of the nations of Europe was prepared to handle the flood of refugees seeking to return to their homes from the camps. This chaos and the massive loss of Jewish life made the establishment of a national homeland in Israel more critical than ever for the survivors. But that desire faced strong opposition.

The British had to deal with growing pressure from the Arab nations to halt the inflow of Jewish refugees into Israel. They established internment camps on the island of Cyprus for Jews who attempted to immigrate to Israel in violation of their policy. The camps operated from August 1946 to January 1949 and in total held about 51,000 persons. Many who survived the Holocaust ended up dying in these camps.

In July of 1947, the British navy intercepted the refugee ship *Exodus* bound for Israel with more than 4,500 Jews on board in international waters. British sailors forcibly boarded the ship, killing two passengers and one crewmember and forced everyone on board to return to Europe. Caught between growing pressure from the Arabs and constant attacks on their police and military from Jewish resistance groups such as the Haganah, Irgun, Lehi and Palmah, the British grew weary trying to keep order. Finally, they turned to the United Nations in hopes of a solution.

On November 29, 1947, the United Nations voted on a partition plan known as UN Resolution 181. This plan, adopted by a vote of 33-13, divided what was then known as Mandate Palestine into two states, one for the Jews and one for the Arabs. The Jewish state was to receive around 56% of the total land area, though it would be separated from Jerusalem, which was designated as an area to be administered by the UN. The plan was accepted by most of the Jewish population, but rejected by the Arabs. This plan was approved to take effect in October of the following year. Before that happened, Great Britain announced they would unilaterally withdraw all troops and officially end the British Mandate on May 14, 1948.

Despite that announcement and their intention to leave, the British refused to hand over any authority or territory to Jewish control ahead of their departure. As a result, the fledgling Israeli government, under the leadership of David Ben-Gurion, was forced to make preparations for the war they knew would follow the British departure. With only a tiny, untrained army and very limited resources, the vastly outnumbered Jewish population turned to supporters in America and other countries to raise the funds needed to purchase arms and military supplies. These contraband items then had to be smuggled into the country.

On May 14, 1948, standing in front of a portrait of Theodor Herzl, Ben-Gurion read Israel's Declaration of Independence that had been approved by the People's Council. The ceremony was broadcast live to the nation on Voice of Israel radio. After all the members present had signed the document, Ben-Gurion declared, "The State of Israel is established!"

The Biblical Borders of Israel

On that day the LORD made a covenant with Abram and said,
"To your descendants I give this land, from the river (wadi) of Egypt to the great river, the Euphrates." ~Genesis 15:18

"I will establish your borders from the Red Sea to the Sea of the Philistines (Mediterranean), and from the desert to the River (Euphrates). ~Exodus 23:31

The LORD said to Moses, "Command the Israelites and say to them: 'When you enter Canaan, the land that will be allotted to you as an inheritance will have these boundaries: "'Your southern side will include some of the Desert of Zin along the border of Edom. On the east, your southern boundary will start from the end of the Salt Sea (Dead Sea), cross south of Scorpion Pass, continue on to Zin and go south of Kadesh Barnea.
Then it will go to Hazar Addar and over to Azmon, where it will turn, join the Wadi of Egypt and end at the Sea(the Mediterranean).
"'Your western boundary will be the coast of the Great Sea (the Mediterranean). This will be your boundary on the west. "'For your northern boundary, run a line from the Great Sea to Mount Hor (Mount Hermon) and from Mount Hor to Lebo[d] Hamath. Then the boundary will go to Zedad, continue to Ziphron and end at Hazar Enan.
This will be your boundary on the north.
"'For your eastern boundary, run a line from Hazar Enan to Shepham. The boundary will go down from Shepham to Riblah on the east side of Ain and continue along the slopes east of the Sea of Kinnereth (Galilee). Then the boundary will go down along the Jordan and end at the Salt Sea. "'This will be your land, with its boundaries on every side."' ~Numbers 34:1-12

A DESPERATE STRUGGLE FOR SURVIVAL

Israel declared its independence on May 14, 1948. That same night, the combined armies of Egypt, Jordan, Iraq, Syria, and Lebanon, along with troops from Saudi Arabia and Yemen invaded Israel. Their stated aim was to create a "United States of Palestine" in place of the Jewish nation established by the UN vote. The invasion was condemned by the United States and other nations as illegal, but it proceeded as thousands of soldiers streamed across the borders.

Arabs living in the new Jewish state were told by Arab leaders in other nations to leave their homes until the Jews could be driven out. They were told it would only be a matter of days or weeks until they could return to their homes.

Often a few hundred Israeli soldiers faced thousands of Arabs. Though outnumbered and outgunned, the Jews fought ferociously for their new homeland. The Israeli Defense Force grew rapidly as civilians joined the fight and immigrants came to Israel by the thousands. By December of 1948 their ranks had grown from less than 30,000 to more than 100,000. The Israeli army focused on protecting Jewish settlements from the invaders and trying to hold their lines to prevent the tiny nation from being broken up into indefensible segments.

Much of the early fighting was inconclusive. Gains of territory by both sides were frequently lost by counterattacks in following days or weeks. Israel gained air superiority with planes purchased from Czechoslovakia, which greatly aided their efforts to repel the invading forces. After nearly a month of fighting, the United Nations brokered a 28-day ceasefire, which took effect on June 11, 1948.

Negotiations made no progress toward achieving a peaceful resolution of the conflict, and on July 8, the day before the ceasefire was to end, Egyptian forces again attacked Israeli positions. Fighting resumed on all fronts for another ten days and Israel made significant territorial gains until a second ceasefire was established on July 18. The second ceasefire lasted until October, although again no progress toward resolution was made during peace talks.

The fighting resumed on October 15 with a massive Israeli assault against Egyptian forces in the Negev Desert that pushed the Egyptian army out of Israel completely. By the end of October, Jewish forces had captured the entire Galilee region and driven Lebanese and Syrian forces out of Israel. Israel continued to realize miraculous military success, and by the end of the year the nation was about one-third larger than it had been when independence was declared. Armistice agreements were signed in the spring of 1949, bringing Israel's first war as a new nation to a close.

Though open fighting ended, there was uneasy peace at best. Terrorist attacks against Israeli civilians—men, women, and children—and population centers continued, and there was a constant threat of war from Israel's larger neighbors. In the mid 1960s the threat of war increased. Egypt signed mutual defense agreements with Syria in 1966 and Jordan in 1967. Jordan also invited Iraqi troops into the country to "protect" against an Israeli attack. Following a false report from Russian intelligence of a pending Israeli offensive, Egypt massed troops on the Sinai border, preparing for an attack of their own.

In early June, Israel discovered plans for a pending coordinated attack from Egypt, Jordan, and Syria. Israeli leaders made the decision to launch a massive preemptive aerial assault. On June 5, 1967, nearly 200 Israeli jets attacked the Egyptian Air Force, virtually wiping it out. Attacks later that day duplicated that success against both Jordan and Syria, guaranteeing Israel air superiority for the remainder of the war.

The ground war that followed was startlingly one-sided. Israeli troops under the command of General Ariel Sharon routed the Egyptians in the Sinai Desert, driving them back all the way across the Suez Canal and capturing the entire peninsula. Jordan attacked Israel after shelling the Jewish sections of Jerusalem, and Israeli troops pushed them back, capturing the West Bank. Following word that the United Nations was about to impose a ceasefire, General Moshe Dayan ordered his troops into the Old City of Jerusalem. On June 7, Israeli paratroopers completed taking control of the entire old city of Jerusalem. Nearly 2,000 years after the Romans captured the Holy City, Jerusalem was once again in Jewish hands.

In the north, Israeli forces succeeded in capturing the strategic Golan Heights region from which Syrian forces had repeatedly shelled Jewish communities in the valley below. By the time the ceasefire was signed on June 11, ending six days of fighting, the size of Israel had tripled. Despite the fact that this entire territory is part of the original land given to Abraham and his descendants by God, Israel's right to hold these "*captured*" areas of the West Bank, Gaza, and the Golan Heights has never been officially recognized by the world community. It is this territory that remains at the core of the current dispute between Israel and the Syrians and Palestinians.

In 1973 the tables were turned as Egypt and Syria launched a surprise attack on Israel during Yom Kippur—the Day of Atonement. On the holiest day of the year for the Jewish People, virtually the entire nation was at a standstill when Egypt and Syria, with participation from Jordan and help from at least nine Arab states, coordinated a massive surprise attack on Israel—from Sinai on the south and the Golan Heights in the north. The initial heavy loss of Israeli soldiers and equipment shocked the Israelis, who had grown confident in their military strength after their earlier successes. Israel was now in grave danger and struggling for her very survival.

After a few days of desperate fighting, Israeli forces brought the invading armies to a halt and began driving them back. In the south, the Israeli counter-attack completely cut off the entire Egyptian Third Army. Only intervention by U.S. Secretary of State Henry Kissinger kept them from being utterly destroyed. Israeli forces crossed the Suez Canal and drove deep into Egypt, at one point reaching a position some 60 miles from Cairo.

At the same time, fighting in the Golan Heights in the north was intense. The Syrian forces there were much closer to Israel's civilian population than were the Egyptian troops in the Sinai. Poorly trained and poorly led, eventually the Syrian troops fled their positions. The Israeli army followed them into Syria, coming as close as 25 miles to the capital of Damascus.

Tensions between the Soviet Union, which supplied and backed the Arab armies, and the United States, which did the same for Israel, escalated. Soviet Premier Leonid Brezhnev threatened to join the war on behalf of Egypt if the Americans did not pressure Israel to accept a ceasefire, which they did on October 25, 1973. As part of the ceasefire agreement, Israel agreed to return the Suez Canal to Egyptian control. Despite the agreements, minor outbreaks of violence continued into the spring of the following year. Israel had narrowly survived the gravest threat she had faced since declaring statehood in 1948.

Israel

1948 to 1967

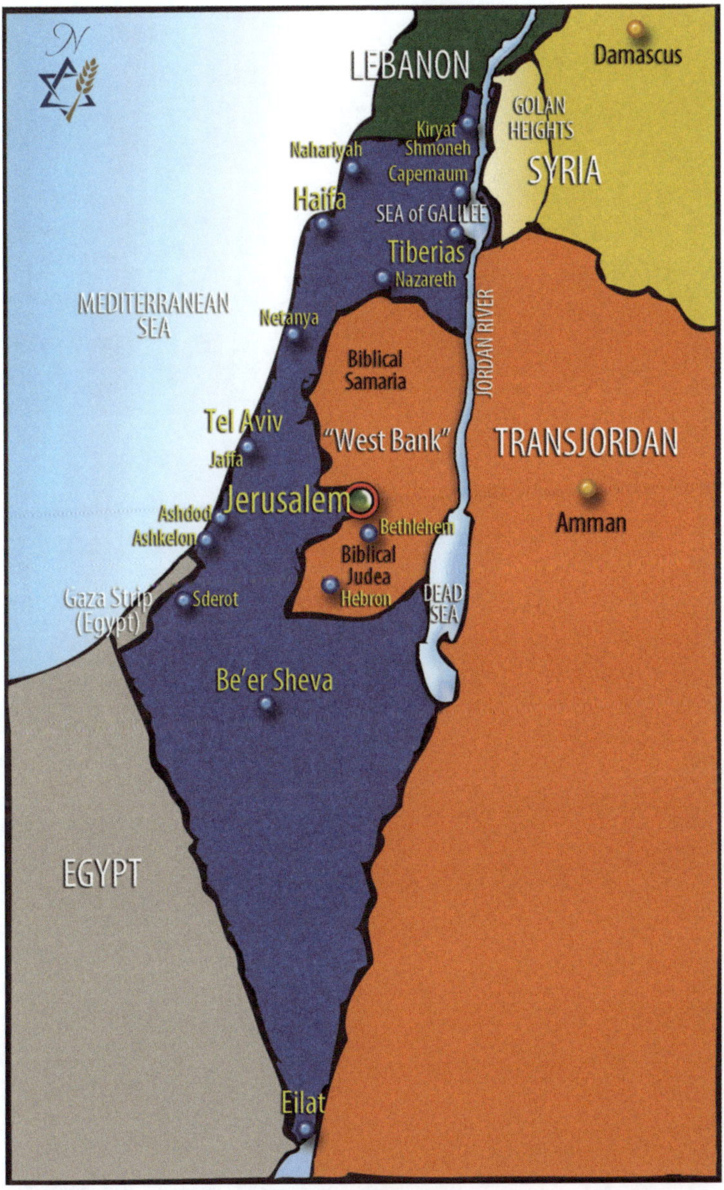

A FRAGILE PEACE

Israel had faced the constant threat of war from her neighbors since her rebirth as a nation in 1948. Outbreaks of actual fighting were punctuated by ceasefires, but there was no real peace. That began to change in the late 1970s when Egypt's President Anwar Sadat made a trip to Israel in 1977. After months of negotiations, and the 1978 Camp David meetings of U.S. President Jimmy Carter, Egyptian President Sadat, and Israel Prime Minister Menachem Begin, Egypt became the first Arab nation to formally recognize Israel's existence and a peace treaty was signed on March 26, 1979.

Israel agreed to completely withdraw from the Sinai Peninsula, which they had captured in 1967 and return it to Egypt. Israel gave up settlements and oil drilling rigs and the millions of dollars of investment they had put in place to develop the Sinai. In return Israel received free right of passage for ships through the Suez Canal. The Sinai was kept as a demilitarized zone to prevent it from being used to launch future attacks against Israel. Sadat and Begin would share the Nobel Peace Prize in 1978. The peace treaty normalized relations between Israel and Egypt, and the two countries exchanged ambassadors and became economic and trading partners.

Reaction in the Arab world to the treaty was bitter and vitriolic. The Arab League expelled Egypt from its membership. Palestine Liberation Organization head Yasser Arafat said the "false peace will not last." In October of 1981, soldiers linked to the radical Muslim Brotherhood assassinated Anwar Sadat. His vice president, Hosni Mubarak, who was wounded in the assassination attempt, succeeded him. Mubarak ruled Egypt as a military dictator (despite being referred to as president) for 30 years, until his ouster early in 2011.

To date only one other Arab country is officially at peace with Israel, and that is Jordan. Negotiations between the two nations began in the late 1980s in an effort to resolve the lingering tensions from the Yom Kippur War. Israel had warned Jordan's King Hussein to stay out of the fighting, but he yielded to pressure from his Arab neighbors and joined the war, suffering great losses as a result.

The negotiations were hampered by political considerations in both countries, and it was not until 1994 that Jordan and Israel signed a peace treaty. The treaty established the Jordan River as the border between the nations, and covered other issues such as water rights and mutual efforts to prevent terrorism. The Clinton Administration promised Jordan billions of dollars in debt forgiveness in exchange for their agreement to the treaty.

With the exception of Egypt, the Arab world responded to Jordan with contempt and anger. Hezbollah terrorists launched mortar and rocket attacks against Jewish civilian targets on the day the treaty was to be signed, hoping to disrupt the move toward peace. It is believed that Israel's Mossad intelligence service saved the life of King Hussein from at least one terrorist assassination attempt. On the death of King Hussein from cancer in 1999, his son King Abdullah II took the throne in Amman. He has continued to build trade and economic ties to Israel in the intervening years.

The governments of other Arab nations have had a complicated relationship with Israel over the years. Some, such as Syria and Iraq, have been extremely hostile. Others such as Saudi Arabia, while internally expressing anger toward the "Zionists" find Israel useful in restraining the same terrorists who threaten their own rule. Perhaps the most interesting case study in the shifting nature of relationships in the Middle East is Iran. Under the Shah, Iran was very friendly to Israel. Today under President Ahmadinejad, Iran represents what is perhaps Israel's greatest threat.

Though there have been other conflicts, including Israel's wars in Lebanon in 1982 and 2006 as well as military operations in Gaza, there has not been another multi-front war such as Israel faced so often during her early years. As part of its constant preparation to respond to threats, service in the Israeli Defense Forces is mandatory for all Israeli citizens when they reach 18 years of age. Aside from exemptions on religious grounds or physical inability, men serve three-year terms and women two-year terms. After their term of regular service, the men must remain active in the reserves. This provides Israel with a large pool of trained personnel should another war break out. Israel has been forced to live by the motto expressed by the Roman military historian Vegetius "Si vis pacem, para bellum"—if you wish for peace, prepare for war.

THE PALESTINIAN QUESTION

When the Arab nations invaded Israel in 1948, they instructed Palestinians living in the newly created Jewish state to flee their homes to neighboring countries. Most expected Israel to be quickly defeated. "You'll be home in a week," many were told. When the war to destroy Israel proved unsuccessful, many thousands were left as refugees. Rather than absorb them into their own populations, Israel's Arab neighbors maintained these people in perpetual refugee status. More than 60 years later, many of these people and their descendants still live in "temporary" camps.

At a 1964 Arab League summit in Cairo, a new group dedicated to the "liberation of Palestine" through armed struggle, the Palestine Liberation Organization (PLO) was formed. Its original charter stated that "Palestine with its boundaries that existed at the time of the British Mandate is an indivisible territorial unit." It is impossible to correctly understand current events in the Middle East without understanding this background.

The core issue is not borders, refugees, or territories assigned by mandates or won through war. The issue is the very existence of Israel. The Palestinian National Charter of 1964 says, "The claims of historic and spiritual ties between Jews and Palestine are not in agreement with the facts of history." Further, the bulk of the Palestinian Charter clearly describes the "sacred" responsibility of the Palestinian Arabs and the Arab world to engage in "armed struggle" toward the "elimination of Zionism" to "liberate Palestine." This charter, which rejects the right of Israel to exist, has never been changed. In the Arab view, this is not about two states living side by side in peace; it is about one state only, and that state must be Palestine.

At the time the Palestine Liberation Organization was created, the territories under dispute today—the Gaza Strip and the West Bank—were under the control of Egypt and Jordan respectively. Yet neither nation was willing to allow "their" lands to be used for a Palestinian homeland. Only after the 1967 war when Israel captured those regions did they become necessary for a Palestinian state.

The figure most closely identified with the PLO was an Egyptian named Mohammed Yasser Abel Rahman Abdel Raouf Arafat al-Qudwa al-Huesseini, better known as Yasser Arafat, who ran the organization with an iron first from 1969 until his death in 2004. Over that 35 year period, he was personally responsible for the deaths of thousands of Jews and Palestinians as well as amassing a personal fortune in the billions. His corrupt reign was a disaster for the Palestinian people, but he continues to be viewed by them as a hero.

The PLO was a terrorist organization from the beginning. The event that first brought them to public consciousness around the world was the 1972 attack on the Israeli athletes at the Olympic Games in Munich by the Black September wing of the PLO. Eleven Israeli coaches and athletes were murdered in the initial raid and the subsequent botched rescue attempt of the survivors.

Though Arafat supposedly spoke for the Palestinian people, he was very unpopular with Arab leaders. King Hussein of Jordan expelled him in a series of bloody armed struggles in 1970-1971 after the PLO was linked to attempts to assassinate him. It is estimated that perhaps as many as 5,000 people died in those battles. Following his ouster, Arafat set up a base of operations in Lebanon, from which he continued to launch attacks against Israel.

In 1982 the Israeli army invaded southern Lebanon in an attempt to destroy the bases the PLO was using to strike at Israel. The PLO had armed itself with thousands of missile and rocket launchers and was striking northern Israel with artillery fire on a near-daily basis. The Israeli army quickly drove the PLO out of their positions in southern Lebanon, and surrounded them in Beirut. When the Syrian air force tried to intervene, the Israeli Air Force shot down more than 80 Syrian planes without suffering a single loss of their own.

The United States stepped in and brokered a ceasefire and right of passage agreement, which allowed Arafat and his fighters to relocate to Tunisia. Arafat remained there until 1993. He survived a number of internal power struggles within the organization and at least one Israeli bombing of his headquarters in Tunis. Arafat continued to call for a Palestinian state and to support terrorist activity, but he also launched a diplomatic initiative to gain recognition and funding from the world community.

Following the Oslo Accords of 1993, Arafat returned to the West Bank, where he established his headquarters in Ramallah. In 1994 Arafat shared the Nobel Peace Prize with Israel's Prime Minister Yitzhak Rabin and President Shimon Peres for the peace treaty. Among the obligations of the treaty, the Palestinians were to recognize Israel's right to exist and put an end to violence. In return, there would be a gradual transition to Palestinian self-rule. Arafat and the PLO never changed their charter to recognize Israel's legitimate right to exist as he promised he would, nor did they put an end to the violence.

Arafat's obsession with the complete destruction of Israel was clearly demonstrated at the Camp David peace talks held by President Clinton in 2000. Israel's Prime Minister, Ehud Barak offered to give Arafat all of Gaza, 94% of the West Bank and most of Jerusalem. It was a much larger concession than anyone expected, but to the shock and amazement of those present, including Mr. Clinton, Arafat turned down the deal.

Arafat continued to play both sides of the fence, convincing Western leaders that he was committed to peace while at the same time continuing to orchestrate terrorist attacks against Jewish civilian and military targets. Arafat successfully used his credentials as a peacemaker to solicit billions in aid from the West. Despite all the funds that were sent to improve the lives of Palestinians, most of the people continued to live in abject poverty. Arafat claimed that the Palestinian Authority was bankrupt, yet a General Accounting Office study run by the United States indicated he had diverted perhaps $10 billion to various Swiss accounts under his personal control.

Arafat fell ill in 2004 and died while being treated in Paris. He was followed in office by Mahmoud Abbas (also known as Abu Mazen) who continues as President of the Palestinian Authority despite the fact that his term of office expired in 2009 and no elections have been held. Abbas was personally involved in financing the Black September Munich raid in 1972, though he denies knowing for what purpose the funds would be used.

The question of the future of the Palestinians was set in motion more than 60 years ago when they and the Arab nations of the Middle East rejected the United Nations plan to create Israel and launched a war to destroy the Jewish state. Today they remain a people without a country, and most of them are still committed to the eventual annihilation of Israel.

THE INTIFADAS

Late in 1987, tensions between the Palestinians and the Israelis boiled over in what became known as the first intifada—the uprising. Two days after a Jewish worker was stabbed and killed in Gaza, an Israeli tank transport killed four Palestinians in a traffic accident. Palestinians declared the collision an intentional act of revenge for the earlier murder, which sparked mass rioting as the false rumor spread among the Palestinians of the West Bank, Gaza, and Jerusalem.

Violent mobs filled the streets, burning tires, destroying vehicles and throwing stones and Molotov cocktails at Israeli soldiers trying to maintain order. Rioters also bombed the U.S. Consulate in Jerusalem. A number of Palestinians were killed or wounded during attacks on Jewish troops; another large group was killed by other Palestinians after being accused of collaborating with Israel. It is impossible to get an accurate count of the dead, but it is believed that as many as 2,000 may have died during the six years of sporadic fighting and violence. The staggering unemployment rate, the systematic corruption of the Palestinian Authority government, and the cramped living conditions all contributed to the uprising which continued until the signing of the Oslo Accords in 1993.

The second intifada began in 2000 and was much more deadly. It featured more full-scale military conflicts, resulting in the deaths of an estimated 6,500 Palestinians and more than 1,100 Jews. This uprising began shortly after the failure of the July 2000 Middle East Peace Summit at Camp David where President Clinton had invited Prime Minister Ehud Barak and

Yasser Arafat to move peace negotiations forward. The talks, although hopeful at first, failed to produce any agreement when Arafat refused the major concessions offered by Israel. Evidence uncovered later revealed that Arafat covertly played a role in launching the unrest to try to gain what he could not through negotiations.

During the following six years, off-and-on fighting between Israeli troops and Palestinian militants continued, along with suicide bombing and missile and mortar attacks against Jewish civilian populations. Palestinian claims of Israeli atrocities were found to be baseless, but they helped continue the unrest and violence. An uneasy truce was declared in 2006, which is generally considered to mark the end of the second intifada.

THE UNRAVELING

The autocratic regimes of the Arab Middle East have been rocked to their foundations in 2011 by a series of protests and demonstrations that have seen some governments toppled while others killed their own citizens by the hundreds or even thousands in a desperate attempt to cling to power. Most of the population in these countries live without the basic freedoms and rights we take for granted. As Prime Minister Netanyahu pointed out in his address to Congress in May of 2011, the Arabs who most enjoy full rights and privileges as citizens are those who live in Israel.

The unrest began in Tunisia, which had been ruled by Zine Ben Ali since 1987. An unlicensed street vendor was mistreated by a policewoman, and in response, he set himself on fire in the streets of Sidi Bouzid. When police cracked down on the protesters who took to the streets to oppose the government's restrictions, full-scale riots broke out. First coverage of the events came through postings on Facebook and YouTube. Within days riots broke out across the country, and in January, Ben Ali fled the country for exile in Saudi Arabia, and elections for a new government are currently underway.

News of the overthrow of the government of Tunisia spread rapidly across the Arab world. Modern social media give ordinary people the means to bypass government-controlled media sources that have long been their only source of information. As word filtered out that a dictator had been deposed, not by military force or assassination, but by ordinary people taking to the streets and demanding the rights they have been denied for so long, the idea that change was possible spread like wildfire.

Protests and demands for increased freedoms sprung up in nations across the region. In many cases extremist groups and terrorists used people's longing for freedom and badly needed political and economic reforms to advance their own agendas and gain power. The face of the Middle East is being transformed before our very eyes, posing both new opportunities and along with it, new dangers for the region, most significantly, for Israel.

EGYPT

Hosni Mubarak ruled Egypt for 30 years following the assassination of Anwar Sadat. Under a state of emergency, he headed a military cabal (Mubarak had been a general in the Egyptian Air Force) that governed a nominal democracy. Mubarak was famously harsh in his treatment of all those who opposed his regime. It is believed that thousands were arrested, tortured, and executed without trials or rights during his rule.

The day after Zine Ben Ali fled from Tunisia, the first protests in Egypt broke out in Cairo and Alexandria, and they quickly spread to other cities. Tens of thousands took to the streets to demand free and open elections and the end of the hated state of emergency. There are strong indications that though many of the protestors desired democracy, many others were foreigners brought in by fanatical Muslim groups to help overthrow the government. Mubarak's supporters responded to the largely peaceful protests with violence. It is believed that more than 800 people were killed during the three weeks of protests against the Mubarak regime.

Mubarak's already tense relations with the army worsened as the protests drug on, and army units refused orders to disperse the crowds in Cairo by force. On February 11, 2011, Mubarak was forced from power, and may well face trial for the abuses committed during his rule. It remains unclear what kind of government will emerge after the elections slated for the fall of 2011 (or whether the elections will even occur as scheduled), but it is already certain that Egypt will be much more hostile toward Israel than in the past.

The Muslim Brotherhood, which was banned since 1954, has been recognized as an official political organization under the name of the Freedom and Justice Party and most observers believe they will have by far the largest bloc in the new Parliament after the elections. This will give them effective control over the new government.

Egypt has already opened its border with Gaza, which had been closed following the ascension to power of Hamas in the Gaza Strip. The closure was intended to prevent weapons from being brought into the country to arm Hamas against Israel. Leading presidential candidates have supported "revisiting" the peace treaty with Israel, and massive protests in support of the Palestinians have been a repeated feature in Cairo and other major cities. Trade deals with Israel, including vitally important supplies of oil and natural gas, face an uncertain future. Egypt has the largest military in the Arab world, and a hostile Egypt would present a challenge Israel has not had to face in more than 30 years. Watch for growing hostility toward Israel as Egypt falls to greater influence of Muslim fanatical leadership.

SYRIA

The revolution that spread from Tunisia to Egypt reached Syria as well in January of 2011. In response, the government of Bashar al-Assad, who inherited power from his father in 1999, instituted a harsh military crackdown. It is believed that Syrian soldiers loyal to the regime in Damascus have already killed nearly 1,000 protestors. Although the army so far has shown no signs of abandoning the current regime, the people, despite the bloodshed, have not yet abandoned their efforts to overthrow the government.

The Ba'ath political party has been in power since 1963 and rules the country under a state of emergency similar to the one Mubarak instituted to stay in power in Egypt. Harsh measures against their own citizens are not new to Syria. In 1982 Hafez al-Assad, father of the current President killed as many as 80,000 people in Hama, Syria, when Islamic groups such as the Muslim Brotherhood led an uprising against him.

For many years Syria has been a major supporter of training and supplies to the terrorist group Hezbollah. Their intelligence service was implicated, along with Hezbollah, in the assassination of Lebanon's Prime Minister Rafik Hariri in 2005. Syria, alongside Iran, often uses Hezbollah as a proxy to launch attacks against Israel without suffering direct reprisals. Through the political wing of their Hezbollah puppet regime, Syria and Iran effectively control the government of Lebanon.

Syria has never formally made peace with Israel. They continue to demand the return of the Golan Heights, the strategic region north of Galilee, which Israel captured from them in 1967. The region provides military high ground from which Syria often launched attacks when it controlled the area, as well as crucial water supplies. It is by no means certain that the overthrow of the al-Assad dynasty would improve relations with Israel. Fanatical Islam has strong roots, especially in southern Syria, near the Israeli border, and as has happened in Egypt, any new government might well be even more radicalized by these fanatics. This would result in a more volatile relationship with Israel than currently exists. At least the current Assad government desires to maintain stable political ties with the West and therefore exercises some restraint in dealing with Israel. This restraint would disappear if Syria were to fall into the hands of a radicalized Muslim leadership, possibly leading to an all out war against Israel.

IRAN

Most do not realize that Iran is not an Arab country; they are Persians. In fact, the majority of the Arab World is afraid of Iran and does not want them to have stronger influence in the region. This has strangely worked to Israel's favor. Still, Iran is the greatest threat Israel currently faces from any other nation in the Middle East. The radical theocracy that has ruled the country since the revolution in 1979 is Israel's sworn enemy and has dedicated themselves to Israel's destruction.

Prior to that time, Iran, under the leadership of the Shah, had been friendly to Israel and a staunch ally of the United States. Sadly, President Jimmy Carter sold out the Shah, forcing him to flee the country and find refuge in America. The radical Shiite mullahs that filled the power vacuum in the wake of the Shah's deposition fomented hatred toward the Jewish State. They continue to pursue development of nuclear weapons in an all out effort to fulfill the stated desire of President Mahmoud Ahmadinejad to "wipe Israel off the map."

The protests against the government following the disputed re-election of Ahmadinejad continue despite the reports of election tampering and subsequent protests in 2009. Voting totals released by the ruling party appeared to have been manipulated, including several provinces where reported turnout exceeded 100 percent of the eligible voters. After a government crackdown in 2010, those protests decreased somewhat, but they roared back to life in February of 2011. As was the case in Egypt and Tunisia, social media has played a major roll in the opposition movement.

Iran has been responsible for equipping Hamas and Hezbollah terrorists with hundreds of millions of dollars worth of arms and training to use against Israel. They recently sent two warships, one a supply ship with an undisclosed cargo, through the Suez Canal to Syria. In addition, several disguised shipments of military hardware have been intercepted on their way to Gaza. This activity, although mildly condemned by the UN and other nations, has resulted in little if any actual repercussions.

Israel has repeatedly asked the world community for help in stopping Iran's nuclear weapons program. Though some economic sanctions have been instituted, they are anemic and have been ineffective in deterring their progress. However, a mysterious computer worm (called the Stuxnet virus) suddenly appeared on the scene in late 2010. Strangely, the worm did not threaten ordinary computers, but was written for a very specific control system built by Siemens, the German company that designed and built the systems used by Iran for their nuclear program. The worm actually rendered their computers worthless and for several months, halted work on Iran's centrifuges used for enriching uranium. The worm is one of the most complex in history, and according to experts, required the involvement of hundreds of programmers and could only have been undertaken by a company the size of Microsoft or a country. Most in the know believe that this was a secret project undertaken by Israel with help from the United States.

It is highly unlikely that the UN or any other nation will undertake military action against Iran to stop them from achieving their nuclear goals. Inevitably, Israel will be forced to strike as Iran nears completion of developing such weapons. No one is exactly sure when this will happen, but most agree they are not far off. Iran's pursuit of nuclear weapons to launch against Israel and their already advanced missile technology makes them the greatest threat Israel faces today.

JORDAN

The neighbor with which Israel shares its longest border is the Hashemite Kingdom of Jordan. Jordan has suffered numerous terrorist attacks due to signing a peace treaty with Israel in 1994. Al-Qaeda bombed three hotels in the capital city of Amman in 2005, killing almost 60 people and wounding more than 100 others. In addition, former King Hussein survived numerous assassination attempts, many of them tied to the Palestine Liberation Organization.

The same wave of unrest that touched other Arab countries also came to Jordan in the beginning of 2011. The protestors who took to the streets called for the dismissal of the Prime Minister and for Parliament to be dissolved. Much of the discontent centers on their difficult economic situation. High unemployment coupled with rapidly rising prices for food and gas have created widespread unrest. The government is widely viewed as corrupt and in the pockets of a few wealthy families with no regard for the common people.

In addition, Jordan's perceived pro-Israel stance is not shared by a significant portion of the population in the largely Sunni Muslim country. King Abdullah II, who succeeded his father after his death from cancer in 1999 and was educated in the West, has positioned his nation as an ally of Israel. Anti-Israeli stories are generally kept off the airwaves. Jordan took steps recently to revoke the citizenship of thousands of Palestinians. The move was described as an effort to support the Palestinian's claim to a homeland in the West Bank by blocking any effort from Israel to permanently resettle them in Jordan. Still, it was not met with popular support and has generated further hostility against the Jordanian government.

Jordan abandoned any demands to the West Bank after they were forced out. In fact, they have had very little interest in asserting any further claim to this area since 1967 since the Palestinian population was problematic to them during their rule. Jordan had annexed the region following the end of the first Arab-Israeli war in 1949, although their control was never formally acknowledged by the United Nations. Because of Jordan's close proximity and the length of their shared border, continued good relations between Israel and Jordan are vital to Israel's security. A breakdown of the current peace would be horrific.

TURKEY

Though Turkey has not undergone the same kind of protests that have rocked other nations in the Middle East, the government has undergone a major shift recently, and it is still unclear what will emerge in the coming months. For many years, Israel enjoyed a somewhat friendly relationship with Turkey. Many Israelis traveled to Turkey to take advantage of the inexpensive vacation opportunities and the countries were active trading partners. During Israel's severe drought in 2000, Turkey was the leading provider of water to the Jewish state.

Sadly, relations with Turkey have been breaking down in the last couple of years as Turkey has yielded to the growing influence of Islamic fundamentalism. This has shifted them from being a moderate nation to identifying with the Islamic world and a growing anti-Israel attitude. Turkey has been a major player in the "aid flotillas" that have attempted to break the arms embargo on Gaza. Turkey, under the Ottoman Empire, was at the head of the Muslim world during the golden age of Islam and controlled most of the Middle East, including what is today Israel until they were defeated by England and France in 1917. Some speculate that Turkey will soon emerge as the leader of a revised Islamic empire. What we can say with certainty is that Turkey poses a growing threat to Israel as they move closer toward Muslim domination and Sharia Law.

Israel

June 1967 ~ After Six Day War

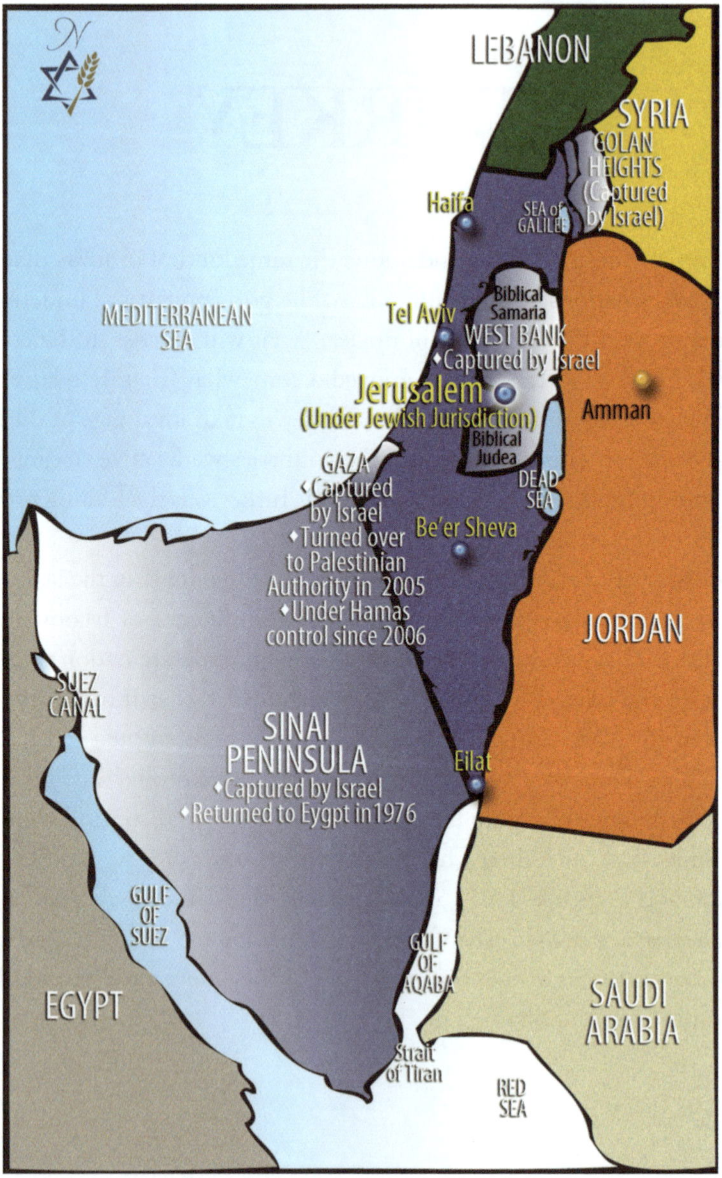

PAST PROPOSALS FOR PEACE

Every U.S. President since Harry Truman has worked to bring peace to the Middle East, but the efforts reached a new level following the conclusion of the 1991 Persian Gulf War. The first Bush Administration, in cooperation with the then Soviet Union, convened a conference in Madrid, Spain, to resolve the Israeli-Arab dispute. It was part of President Bush's vision for a "new world order." Leaders from Israel, Syria, Jordan, Lebanon, and the Palestinians (though not the Palestine Liberation Organization) were invited to attend.

Though the United States had been seen as strongly pro-Israel under President Reagan, the Bush Administration signaled a new willingness to demand concessions from Israel to obtain a peace agreement. The U.S. delayed certain loan guarantees to Israel until Israel agreed to attend the conference. One positive outcome of the Madrid Conference was that Israel successfully lobbied to have UN Resolution 3379, which equated Zionism with racism, revoked.

Madrid produced little else beyond agreement to continue ongoing bilateral and multi-state negotiations. However, the talks did lead to the peace treaty between Israel and Jordan, which was signed in 1994. Otherwise, the positions of the two sides on issues such as the fate of Jerusalem, the "right of return" for Palestinians and security arrangements quickly hardened, and no serious progress was made toward achieving permanent peace.

When President Clinton took office in 1993, he continued the U.S. efforts to produce a lasting peace accord between Israel and the Palestinians. Secret talks between Israel and the PLO were held in Oslo, Norway in August of 1993, and the Oslo Accords were signed at the White House in September. The agreement created the Palestinian Authority, which was intended to form the basis for a future Palestinian government.

The talks called for a gradual transfer of authority to the Palestinians, and a gradual withdrawal of Israeli forces from Gaza and the West Bank. Discussions on the most contentious issues were deferred until later in the process, which was supposed to take no more than five years. The deal was not accepted by all Palestinians, and despite the "official" recognition of Israel by the PLO per a letter from Yasser Arafat, many on both sides viewed that acceptance as a tactic to allow the Palestinians to build up their military strength prior to another offensive against Israel. In fact, in the months following the signing of the Oslo Accords, attacks against Israel increased.

In an effort to produce concrete progress following the expiration of the five year window laid out in the Oslo Accords, President Clinton brought Prime Minister Benjamin Netanyahu and PLO Chief Yasser Arafat together at Wye River in Maryland in 1998. The two men distrusted each other, and Clinton brought in King Hussein of Jordan to help mediate their disagreements. The Wye River Memorandum was meant to provide concrete steps for progress toward Palestinian self-rule and the eventual establishment of a Palestinian state.

Israel was to accelerate withdrawal from part of the West Bank, and in return the PLO was to make the changes to their charter promised in 1993, mainly the recognition of Israel's right to exist. As of 2011, these changes still have never been made. Israel, as promised, began the land transfers but the Palestinians failed to take the reciprocal steps they agreed to in order to promote Israel's security. As a result, the transfers were halted and the Wye River plan faded into obscurity.

The George W. Bush Administration followed and was quickly turned from the Middle East to the War on Terror following the attacks of 9/11. Although this occupied most of his attention and focus, the Israeli-Palestinian issue did not go unnoticed. In 2002, following his military response in Afghanistan, President Bush organized the Quartet—made up of the U.S., the United Nations, the European Union, and Russia—and put together a "road map for peace." Bush described his plan as "a starting point toward achieving the vision of two states, a secure State of Israel and a viable, peaceful, democratic Palestine.

The Israeli government of Ariel Sharon objected to many elements of the plan, and wanted it to include demands to disarm the various Palestinian terrorist organizations, as well as to allow continued building of homes in existing Israeli settlements. Shortly after President Bush attended a major conference in 2003, terrorist activity increased dramatically. Many Palestinian groups refused to acknowledge any agreement that included recognition of Israel's right to exist as a Jewish state.

With none of the steps to reach the goals of the "road map" being taken, President Bush tried again in 2004 to restart negotiations. While acknowledging that his goal of 2005 for the establishment of a Palestinian state would not be possible, Bush nevertheless encouraged the process to continue. The death of Yasser Arafat in November of 2004 changed the dynamics of the talks. In 2005, Israel began a complete withdrawal from Gaza. Meant as a "land for peace" gesture, the withdrawal required the removal of many Israeli citizens from their homes. Rather than producing peace, the withdrawal encouraged the Palestinians that Israel could be defeated. Gaza became a launching ground for thousands of rocket and mortar attacks against southern Israel. Israel's military action against Hamas terrorists in 2008, Operation *Cast Lead*, emphatically ended hopes of progress for the road map.

When President Obama took office, he increased pressure on Israel to make concessions to produce a peace agreement. The Obama Administration has strongly supported the quick creation of a Palestinian state, and insists that East Jerusalem must be the capital of the new nation. In 2011, President Obama created a firestorm when he called for new state to be based on "1967 borders with agreed upon land swaps." This unprecedented demand was announced just as Israel's Prime Minister Benjamin Netanyahu was enroute to the United States for talks with Obama, and created a rather tense situation. Upon arriving in the U.S. and following meetings with the President, he made it clear in a news conference from the White House that these conditions were unacceptable to Israel. It would leave them with indefensible borders that would threaten the security and very survival of Israel.

In a polite but firm lecture, he made it clear to our President and the world that the Jewish People have been persecuted throughout history, losing six million in the Holocaust while no nation came to their aid. Israel was established as a sanctuary to insure that this would never happen again and so under no circumstances would he allow the continued existence of Israel to be jeopardized. In a speech to the joint House of Representatives several days later, he reaffirmed Israel's position and unwillingness to return to the 1967 borders. He received thunderous applause throughout his speech reaffirming that Israel still has significant support within our Congress.

The Palestinians announced their plan to seek United Nations recognition at the UN General Assembly in September of 2011. More than 100 nations have already established some diplomatic relations with the Palestinians, and the measure is expected to receive overwhelming support. Such an action would allow the Palestinians to pursue claims against Israel in various international courts and tribunals. In addition, by receiving recognition as a nation unilaterally, the Palestinians have stated that they believe they will gain more than they could through negotiations with Israel.

THE PALESTINIANS TODAY

The two Palestinian land areas, Gaza and the West Bank, have never been part of a single nation. Prior to the 1967 Six Day War, they were governed separately by Egypt and Jordan. There are a little over 1.5 million Palestinians living in Gaza and approximately 2.5 million in the West Bank. Though they have been technically under a democratic government since the Oslo Accords in 2003, the most recent scheduled elections have been canceled, and President Mahmoud Abbas has remained in office for more than two years past the conclusion of his term.

The Palestinian political scene is splintered, but the two main political parties are Fatah and Hamas. Fatah is the party more closely aligned with Yasser Arafat's ideology (ironically they are considered to be the "moderate" party) while Hamas is linked to the radical Muslim Brotherhood and Islamic Jihad groups. Bitter fighting between the two parties has been common, and it is believed that at least several hundred Palestinians have been killed in disputes between the two.

In the elections for the Palestinian Legislative Council held in 2006, Hamas gained a large majority in the body, holding 74 seats compared to 45 for Fatah. The election produced a seismic shift in international relations. Because Hamas is identified as a terrorist organization, the Quartet—the U.S., the United Nations, the European Union, and Russia—imposed economic sanctions on the Palestinian Authority, greatly crippling their economy. The fact that the Palestinians had elected a terrorist organization that continues to insist on the destruction of the Jewish State to head their government made it impossible for Israel, to consider any further concessions or negotiations with them.

In 2007, the Gaza War between Hamas and Fatah factions broke out. With Israel and the United States supporting the government of Mahmoud Abbas (a Fatah leader) to strengthen his position against his more radical opponents, Palestinians linked to Hamas claimed he was a "puppet" of foreign interests. Hamas fighters drove out all Fatah officials from Gaza, killed more than 100, and wounded at least 500 others. Since then, Hamas effectively rules Gaza, from which Israel completely withdrew in 2005, and Fatah rules the West Bank.

A recent reconciliation between Fatah and Hamas took place in April 2011 in Egypt. This agreement between the two rival groups will likely strengthen their position in the E.U., UN, and perhaps even in the U.S. Netanyahu has stated this represents a setback for Israel since an Hamas-led government now supported by the Palestinian Authority is not a viable partner for negotiation. In order for any negotiations to go forward, the Palestinian Authority must disassociate themselves from Hamas, a terrorist organization and sworn enemy of Israel.

IS PEACE POSSIBLE?

One of Israel's greatest Prime Ministers, Golda Meir, once said, "Peace will come when the Arabs love their children more than they hate us." Since Israel's statehood in 1948, they have endured repeated wars and attacks. They have constantly faced the threat of a hostile Arab world that wants it gone. Thousands of their young soldiers have been killed in this struggle for their survival and thousands more civilians have perished in terrorist attacks and suicide bombings.

Despite decades of negotiations and numerous accords and agreements, things have not changed all that much between Israel and the Palestinians over the last 40+ years. In fact, the prospect of peace today seems further away than ever. Israel presently has no viable partner with whom they can seriously negotiate. An Hamas-led Palestinian government is certainly not an option. The Obama administration is clearly no longer able to play the role of "impartial" mediator in this conflict now that a demand to return to the pre-1967 borders has been announced.

The rise to power of radical Islamic groups like the Muslim Brotherhood in Egypt, particularly given their historic ties to Hamas and their hatred of Israel, coupled with continued terrorist activity from Hamas and Hezbollah and the looming specter of Iran's nuclear weapons program have created the greatest threat to Israel's continued existence they have faced since the Yom Kippur war of 1973. In addition, long-time allies such as Great Britain and the United States have recently shifted position and taken a more adversarial role toward Israel, indicating a willingness to accept a

Hamas-led Palestinian government and overlooking that they are a terrorist organization. The post 9-11 days of "we don't negotiate with terrorists" seem to be fading.

Israel is a tiny nation—the entire country could fit inside the borders of Lake Michigan with room to spare. Surrounded by enemies on every side and greatly outnumbered by her Arab neighbors, the survival of Israel from 1948 to the present is surely a result of Divine Providence and staggering sacrifice on the part of generation after generation of Israelis.

As you hear and see Israel being pressed to make concessions of land for peace, keep in mind that all of the concessions made to date have only been met with demands for more, and have resulted not in peace but in continued hostility. If the Palestinians truly wanted to live in peaceful co-existence with Israel, then Gaza—turned over to them in 2005—would today be engaged in trade with Israel and living in friendship side by side. Instead, Gaza has become a staging ground for almost daily missile attacks launched against nearby Israeli towns. Why would we expect anything different if Israel gives over the entire West Bank?

The lessons of the last century should have taught us that appeasement never works, but it appears that our generation is intent on relearning that lesson at Israel's expense. Truth be told, it is highly unlikely if not impossible that any plan for peace engineered or imposed by man will succeed. The only viable plan for peace that **will** succeed is God's peace plan, and that plan is through the Prince of Peace, Yeshua—Jesus, the Messiah. Only when He is invited in and hearts are changed can Arab and Jew, Israeli and Palestinian live in true peace with one another.

HOW SHOULD WE RESPOND?

It is important as Bible believers that we always remember that it is a spiritual issue, not a political issue. Our understanding of this conflict and how we should respond must be rooted in the Word of God. What God says matters far more than what man says or thinks. We must turn to the Scriptures and align ourselves with God's perspectives on such issues. In Genesis 15:18, God promised the Land of Israel—far more than the modern boundaries as you can see from the map at the end of this section—to Abraham and his descendants as an everlasting possession. *"On the same day the LORD made a covenant with Abram, saying: 'To your descendants I have given this land, from the river of Egypt to the great river, the River Euphrates.'"* God confirmed that promise through Moses when the Children of Israel were ready to enter the Promised Land. Deuteronomy 1:8 says, *"See, I have set the land before you; go in and possess the land which the LORD swore to your fathers—to Abraham, Isaac, and Jacob—to give to them and their descendants after them."*

Support for Israel does not mean we believe God loves Jews more than Arabs or Israelis more than Palestinians. It is simply a recognition that God, in His sovereignty, chose to give this land to the Children of Israel. It is their inheritance, regardless of their spiritual condition. That purpose has not changed; indeed, it cannot be abolished by the will or actions of men. Although Jerusalem and the Temple were destroyed almost 2,000 years ago, and the People scattered to four corners of the earth, ties to the land have never been broken. Through the centuries of exile, there has always been a Jewish presence in the land, and the restoration of Israel and Jerusalem as her capital has remained central in the hearts and prayers of the Jewish People.

They are to dwell again in this land after God restores them a second time (see Isaiah 11:11 and Deuteronomy 30:4) and, in fact, do not have the right to give this land away to anyone. Israel was to be a physical sign to the world of God's faithfulness to the truth of His Word. The restoration of the Jewish People to their land and their re-gathering from all the nations to which they were scattered is a clear fulfillment of Bible prophecy connected to the Last Days and signals the near return of Yeshua to this earth.

When we understand this and how this all connects to God's plan for the redemption of mankind, we should be motivated to pray regularly for Israel. Psalm 122:6 exhorts us to *"pray for the peace of Jerusalem: they shall prosper that love thee"* (KJV). The word *peace* is the Hebrew word, ***shalom***:

שָׁלוֹם

It perhaps can best be translated as "completion or wholeness." My understanding of this verse is that when we pray for *the peace of Jerusalem,* we should actually be praying for God's plan to be brought to completion or fullness for both the land and the People of Israel. And that plan ultimately is (as I mentioned above) for the revelation of His Son to come into the hearts of Jews and Arabs alike.

We should pray for those who hate Israel and the Jewish People to be thwarted in their efforts to bring death and destruction. We should pray that God opens the eyes of world leaders to understand the Word of God and to stand with Israel. We should pray for Israel's leaders, for wisdom and divine revelation. We should pray for their salvation and the salvation of all Israel—that the day will come when they cry out, *"Blessed is He who comes in the Name of the Lord"* (Psalm 118:26).

We should speak out, making our voices heard on this extremely important issue. If we remain silent, we are allowing those who seek the destruction of Israel to dominate the discussion. We abdicate not only our rights, but in fact, our divine mandate to "occupy until He comes and make our voices heard." Centuries ago Edmund Burke said, "The only thing necessary for evil to triumph is for good men to do nothing." The current Prime Minister of Israel, Benjamin Netanyahu, has repeatedly expressed his appreciation for the support Israel has received from Christians in America and other nations. Those of us who know the truth have a special responsibility to do what we can to help shape the debate and public opinion and to counter the often-misleading information and propaganda that fills the airwaves.

There are many physical needs in Israel today, as the constant threat of terror attacks and repeated economic boycotts continue. Israel has absorbed over 1,000,000 Russian-speaking Jews and approximately 130,000 Ethiopian Jews in recent years and that has taken its economic toll as well. Many live in desperate poverty, including tens of thousands of Holocaust survivors. For many of these people, the only outside help and encouragement they receive is from Believers who give sacrificially to help meet their needs. We at Jewish Voice have been very involved in reaching out to these hurting people in real and practical ways and have invested hundreds of thousands of dollars to provide for their needs with the help of our partners.

Finally and most important, we must be diligent in our efforts to proclaim the Good News that Yeshua is the promised Messiah of Israel. He is God's solution to this age-old conflict, the only solution that will succeed. Romans 11 clearly teaches that God is not finished with the Jewish People. He has not, nor will He ever reject them. He remains faithful and declares the day will come before Yeshua returns when the blindness that has covered their eyes for almost 2,000 years will finally be lifted, culminating in that glorious day when *"all Israel shall be saved"* (Romans 11:26, KJV). While we can and should pray for and speak out in support of Israel, our most important contribution to the Jewish People is to share with them the Gospel, to prepare them for that blessed day when they will greet Yeshua and claim Him as their Messiah.

Israel

2011 Current Disputed Borders

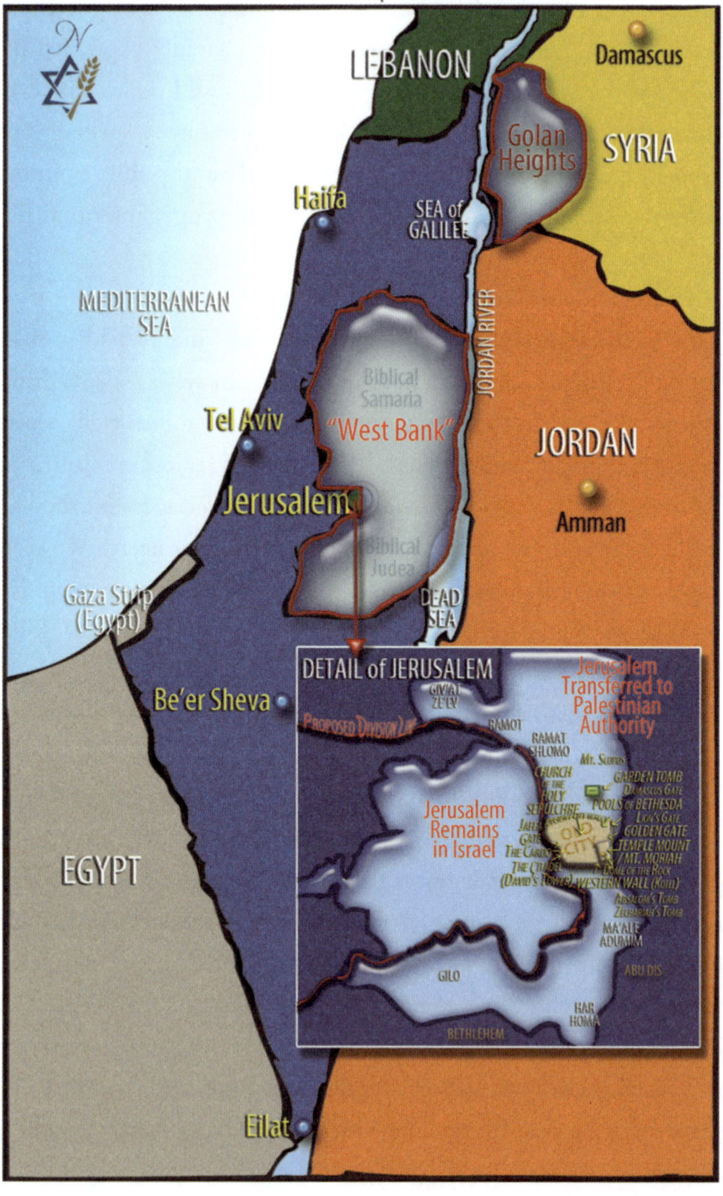